饮水思源
中国人的信仰根源

The True Spiritual Roots for All Chinese
"When you drink water, remember the source"

简体版
作者：董大源，裴瑞明
研究指导：Dr. Hoover Wong
Copyright © 2015 董大源，裴瑞明

Author: Davy Tong, Dr. Raymond Paul Petzholt
Research Mentor: Dr. Hoover Wong
Editing Staff: Alison Tong, Mallory Fu, Annie Petzholt
Copyright © 2015. Davy Tong and Raymond Petzholt

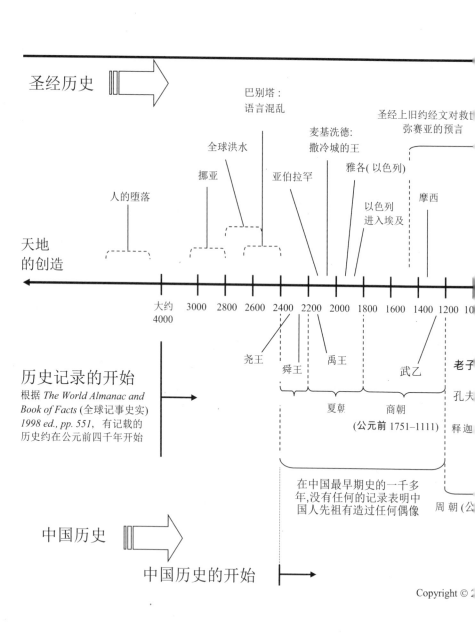

圣经历史

巴别塔:
语言混乱

圣经上旧约经文对救世
弥赛亚的预言

全球洪水

麦基洗德:
撒冷城的王

挪亚

亚伯拉罕

雅各(以色列)

人的堕落

以色列
进入埃及

摩西

天地
的创造

大约
4000　3000　2800　2600　2400　2200　2000　1800　1600　1400　1200　10

尧王

舜王

禹王

武乙

老子

历史记录的开始

根据 *The World Almanac and
Book of Facts* (全球记事史实)
1998 ed., pp. 551, 有记载的
历史约在公元前四千年开始

夏朝

商朝

(公元前 1751–1111)

孔夫

释迦

在中国最早期史的一千多
年,没有任何的记录表明中
国人先祖有造过任何偶像

周朝(公

中国历史

中国历史的开始

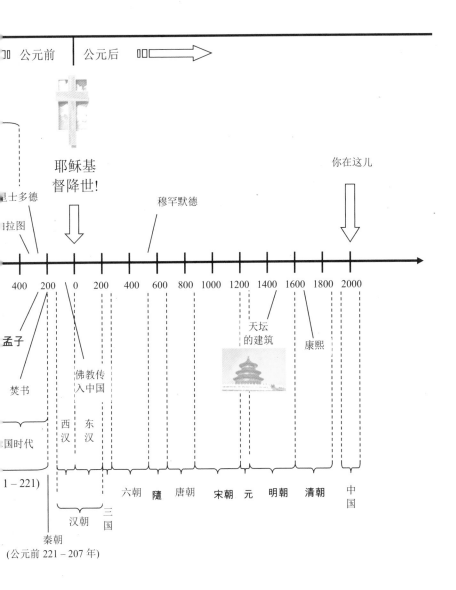

公元前　公元后

耶稣基督降世!

穆罕默德

你在这儿

亚里士多德

柏拉图

400　200　0　200　400　600　800　1000　1200　1400　1600　1800　2000

孟子

焚书

佛教传入中国

天坛的建筑

康熙

西汉　东汉

国时代

1 – 221)

六朝　隨　唐朝　宋朝　元　明朝　清朝　中国

汉朝　三国

秦朝

(公元前 221 – 207 年)

The Chinese Person's True Spirit

Biblical and Western History

Ol
Conce

The Fall of Man

Global Flood

Tower of Babel:
Confusion of Languages

Noah

Abraham

Melchizedek, king of Sale

Jacob

Nation of Israel
Enters Egypt

Creation
of the
Universe

Approx.
4000

3000 2800 2600 2400 2200 2000 1800 1600 1400

King Yao 堯

King Yu 禹

King Shun 舜

King Wu Yi 武乙

The Beginnings
of Recorded History

According to *The World Almanac*
and Book of Facts(1998, pp.551),
recorded history begins
approximately 4000 B.C.

Legendary
Period   Xia/Hsia
夏 Dynasty
(2183 – 1751 BC)

Shang 商 Dynasty
(1751 – 1111 B

Chinese History

The Beginnings of
Chinese History

For over 1,000 years, there was no
known record of the Chinese ever
fashioning any idol images.

Z
V

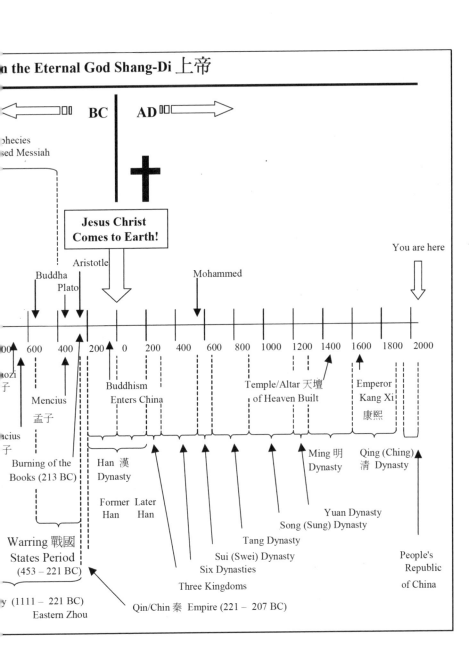

n the Eternal God Shang-Di 上帝

BC | AD

phecies
sed Messiah

Jesus Christ Comes to Earth!

You are here

Aristotle

Buddha
Plato

Mohammed

600 400 200 0 200 400 600 800 1000 1200 1400 1600 1800 2000

ozi
子

Mencius
孟子

Buddhism
Enters China

Temple/Altar 天壇
of Heaven Built

Emperor
Kang Xi
康熙

cius
子

Burning of the
Books (213 BC)

Han 漢
Dynasty

Ming 明
Dynasty

Qing (Ching)
清 Dynasty

Former Later
Han   Han

Yuan Dynasty

Song (Sung) Dynasty

Tang Dynasty

Warring 戰國
States Period
(453 – 221 BC)

Sui (Swei) Dynasty

Six Dynasties

People's
Republic
of China

Three Kingdoms

y (1111 – 221 BC)
Eastern Zhou

Qin/Chin 秦 Empire (221 – 207 BC)

Preface

Purpose of this Booklet

Are you Chinese? Do you know where your true roots really are: as a Chinese and as a person? Do you know why you are here on this earth and how you got here? The purpose of this booklet is to explain, through the study of factual history, the true spiritual and religious roots of the Chinese people. Are your true spiritual roots found in Buddhism, Taoism, Confucianism, Atheism, or even Christianity!? You will find out the exciting answers to these questions and more in this booklet!

A note to the Reader

All information presented in this booklet has been thoroughly researched and documented. A large portion of the information contained in this booklet is taken from several scholarly sources, including:

1) The *Shu Jing* 書經, or Book of History compiled by Confucius.

For centuries since the time of Confucius, the *Si Shu Wu Jing* 四書五經 served as the "Bible" of Chinese thought. Until recent times, they were widely studied and revered. Of the five books included in the *Chinese Classics,* the most often referenced to in this pamphlet is the *Shu Jing* 書經, or 尚書, the *Book of History* or *Book of Documents,* compiled by Confucius. Much of what we know about the early beginnings of Chinese civilization comes from the records contained within the *Shu Jing*. Its historical account spans from the legendary period, the earliest times of Chinese history, to the middle of the Zhou/Chou 周 Dynasty.

2.) *The Notions of the Chinese Concerning God and Spirits* by James Legge

This book covers topics concerning Chinese beliefs and concepts concerning the terms for God 上帝 and spirits 神. Though he was a westerner Legge was considered one of the greatest Chinese scholars of his time, even among the Chinese scholars themselves! Legge gives us an account of the Ming emperors, and their reasons for building the Temple/Altar of Heaven 天壇, located in present-day Beijing.

前言

小册子的目的

你是中国人吗？作为一个人，一个中国人，你知不知道你真正的根本从何而来？你知不知道你为何会活在世上，而且你是怎么来的呢？本册子的目的是从历史的比较和沿革中去寻找中国人属灵信仰的真正根源。我们信仰的根源是来自佛教、道教、孔教、无神论，甚或基督教呢？阅读完这本册子将能精彩地帮助我们解答以上那些问题！

给读者的说明

本册子的资料全部经过深入研究并根据史实的记载，主要材料来自以下几本学术文献：

1. 《书经》

自孔子以来的所多世纪，《四书五经》一直是中国人思想的基本《圣经》；直到近代，它们还广受研读和敬重。在中国古典文学中由孔子所编撰的《书经》（也称为《尚书》），是本册子所引用最多的。《书经》记录了许多中华早期的文化和文明，它所记录的历史故事，时间溯自上古史传说时代，一直到周朝中期。

2. The Notions of the Chinese Concerning God and Spirits
（中国人对上帝和神的看法，理雅各 James Legge 著）

此书对中国人对上帝和神明的信仰和观念作了广泛的讨论。作者理雅各虽为西方人，却被公认为他那时代，包括华人学者在内，最伟大的汉文化学者之一。他在本书中对明朝皇帝建筑现位于北京天坛的原因，作了深入的说明。

3.) The *Holy Bible*

The *Holy Bible* consists of a total of 66 books. The most often referenced to within this booklet is the book of *Genesis*. Here we find a record of our roots as human beings. Most pre-Chinese history is taken from this book. Of all the references and resources used to compile this pamphlet, the *Holy Bible* is the only book that claims to be divinely inspired.

The chronological time chart in the front of this booklet (based on Bishop James Ussher's *The Annals of the World*) will help you follow the flow of time and fully grasp the importance of the historical events and people described within this booklet. The Chinese chronology is based on Herbert A. Giles' *A Chinese-English Dictionary*.

Creation of the Heavens and the Earth

God created the heavens and the earth. This means that space, matter, and even time itself had a beginning. The history of the universe begins here.

> *"In the beginning, God created the heaven and the earth."*   Genesis 1:1

The Beginnings of Recorded History

According to *The World Almanac and Book of Facts (1998 ed., pp. 551)*, recorded history begins approximately 4,000 BC. This matches well with the beginning of recorded history in the Bible, beginning with the account of Adam and Eve. According to God's Word, the Bible, you are specially created for a special purpose!

This means that God has planned a glorious destiny for you! Continue reading to find out more about this exciting destiny!

> *"And the LORD God formed man of the dust of the ground, and breathed into his nostrils the breath of life; and man became a living soul."*   Genesis 2:7

> *"And hath made of one blood all nations of men for to dwell on all the face of the earth, and hath determined the times before appointed, and the bounds of their habitation; That they should seek the Lord, if haply they might feel after him, and find him, though he be not far from every one of us."*   Acts 17:26-27

3. 《圣经》

　　《圣经》有六十六卷书，其中《创世记》是本册子最常引用的书卷。《创世记》记载了人类的始源，大部份在中国记史以前的历史，都来自这卷书。在本册子所引用的所有文献中，只有《圣经》自称是来自上帝的默示。

　　本册子首页附历史时间表（依据詹母士亚薛 James Ussher, The Annals of the World 的世界年表），以帮助读者明白本册中所描述的重要历史人物和事件的时间次序。中华年代表依据的是 Herbert A. Giles 的中英文字典。

天地的创造

　　上帝创造了天地，这表示空间、物质，甚至时间都有起点。宇宙的历史从这时开始。

　　「起初，上帝创造了天地。」　　　　　　　创世记1:1

历史记录的开始

　　根据 The World Almanac and Book of Facts（全球记事史实，1998 ed.，pp.551），有文字记载的历史约在公元前四千年开始，这正好与《圣经》记述亚当、夏娃的被造吻合。根据《圣经》-上帝的话语，人的创造是有特别的目的的。这就是说上帝为你我安排了美好的前程！请继续阅读下去吧！

　　「耶和华神用地上的尘土造人，将生气吹在他鼻孔里，他就成了有灵的活人。」　　　　　　　创世记2:7

　　「他从一本造出万族的人，住在全地上，并且预先定准他们的年限和所住的疆界。要叫他们寻求神，或者可以揣摩而得，其实他离我们各人不远。」

　　　　　　　　　　　　　　　　　　使徒行传17:26，27

"I will praise thee; for I am fearfully and wonderfully made: marvelous are thy works; and that my soul knoweth right well."   Psalms 139:14

We see here that from the very beginning, we were a special creation, unlike monkeys or apes.

The Fall of Man

Shortly after their creation, Adam and Eve disobeyed God. As a result of their sin, death and suffering were brought into the world.

"Wherefore, as by one man [Adam] sin entered the world, and death by sin; and so death passed upon all men, for that all have sinned."
Romans 5:12

"For the wages of sin is death; but the gift of God is eternal life through Jesus Christ our Lord."   Romans 6:23

"For all have sinned, and come short of the glory of God." Romans 3:23

"The heart is deceitful above all things, and desperately wicked..."
Jeremiah 17:9

Noah

Many generations after Adam, people became extremely corrupt and violent in the sight of the LORD God.   So the righteous Creator had to send a Global Flood as judgment for man's wickedness.   In those days, there was one man by the name of Noah who was righteous in God's sight. God therefore spared Noah's life, and the lives of his family members.   God commanded Noah to build an ark large enough to house his own family and to take aboard at least two (male and female) of each kind of land and air animal.

"And GOD saw that the wickedness of man was great in the earth, and that every imagination of the thoughts of his heart was only evil continually. And it repented the LORD that he had made man on the earth, and it grieved him at his heart. And the LORD said, I will destroy man whom I have created from the face of the earth; both man, and beast, and the creeping thing, and the fowls of the air; for it repenteth me that I have made them. But Noah found grace in the eyes of the LORD."   Genesis 6:5-8

「我要称谢祢，因我受造，奇妙可畏；祢的作为奇妙，这是我心深知道的。」 诗篇 139:14

由此可见我们从起初就是特别地被创造，与猴子是绝对不一样的!

人的堕落

亚当、夏娃被造后不久就违背上帝。他们犯罪的结果将死亡与苦难带到世界上。

「这就如罪是从一人入了世界，死又是从罪来的，于是死就临到众人，因众人都犯了罪。」 罗马书 5:12

「因为罪的工价乃是死；惟有上帝的恩赐，在我们的主基督耶稣里，乃是永生。」 罗马书 6:23

「因为世人都犯了罪，亏缺了上帝的荣耀。」 罗马书 3:23

「人心比万物诡诈，坏到极处，谁能识透呢?」 耶利米书 17:9

挪亚

亚当之后过了许多世代，人类腐败到极点，行上帝眼中看为邪恶的事，因此公义的创造主差遣全球洪水来审判人类的罪恶。那时有一个人名叫挪亚，他在上帝眼中看来是公义的，所以上帝要拯救他和他全家免于死亡。上帝吩咐挪亚建一个足够安置他家人及至少一对各种地上走兽和空中飞鸟的方舟。

「耶和华见人在地上罪恶很大，终日思想的尽都是恶，耶和华就后悔造人在地上，心中忧伤。耶和华说：『我要将所造的人和走兽，并昆虫，以及空中的飞鸟，都从地上除灭，因为我造他们后悔了。』唯有挪亚在耶和华面前蒙恩。」 创世纪 6:5—8

"And God said unto Noah, The end of all flesh is come before me; for the earth is filled with violence through them; and, behold, I will destroy them with the earth. Make thee an ark of gopher wood...."

Genesis 6:13-14

The Global Flood

The Flood that God sent was his righteous judgment on man's wickedness, and it killed all land and air creatures, as well as all people. Only the animals and people aboard Noah's ark were saved. These people included Noah, his three sons Shem, Ham, and Japheth, and their wives: a total of eight people. After the flood waters had receded, Noah, his family, and all the animals exit the ark. Noah then built an altar and offered burnt sacrifices to the God of Heaven for His mercy, grace, and for saving his entire family. It is noteworthy that the Chinese have a very similar custom of offering burnt sacrifices to the Supreme Being whom they call Shang-Di 上帝. This custom extends to the very beginnings of Chinese civilization. We will take a closer look at this later.

"And Noah went in, and his sons, and his wife, and his sons' wives with him, into the ark, because of the waters of the flood." Genesis 7:7

"And the waters prevailed exceedingly upon the earth; and all the high hills, that were under the whole heaven, were covered. Fifteen cubits upward did the waters prevail; and the mountains were covered. And all flesh died that moved upon the earth, both of fowl, and of cattle, and of beast, and of every creeping thing that creepeth upon the earth, and every man." Genesis 7:19-21

"And Noah builded an altar unto the LORD; and took of every clean beast, and of every clean fowl, and offered burnt offerings on the altar. And the LORD smelled a sweet savour..." Genesis 8:20-21

Tower of Babel

After the Flood, God commanded man to multiply, spread, and repopulate the whole earth. At this point in human history, mankind spoke only one language, had only one national government, and were united under one culture. Because of man's sinful nature, the people took advantage of this unprecedented unity to rebel against their Creator God. They did so by refusing to spread out and attempted to build a tower, located in ancient Babel, whose top would "reach the heavens." Because of their rebellion, God forced mankind to scatter across the

「上帝就对挪亚说：凡有血气的人，他的尽头已经来到我面前；因为地上满了他们的强暴，我要把他们和地一并毁灭。你要用歌斐木造一只方舟……」

创世记 6:13-14

全球洪水

上帝所差遣的洪水是祂对世人的邪恶公义的审判，将地上和天空一切生物，包括人类都除灭。只有在挪亚方舟上的人和生物蒙拯救。这些人包括挪亚夫妻、他们的三个儿子闪，含，雅弗，以及他们的妻子，总共八人。洪水退后，挪亚和家眷与动物都出了方舟。挪亚建了一座祭坛，献燔祭给上帝，感谢祂的怜悯、恩惠，以及救命之恩。值得一提的是，中国人也有一个十分类似对至高上帝的献祭习俗，这个习俗自中国文明初期就已存在，我们在后文中会作解说。

「挪亚就同他的妻和儿子、儿妇，都进入方舟，躲避洪水。」

创世记 7:7

「水势在地上极其浩大，天下的高山都淹没了。水势比山高过十五肘，山岭都淹没了。凡在地上有血肉的动物，就是飞鸟、牲畜、走兽，和爬在地上的昆虫，以及所有的人，都死了。」

创世记 7:19-21

「挪亚为耶和华筑了一座坛，拿各类洁净的牲畜，飞鸟献在坛上为燔祭，耶和华闻那馨香之气……」

创世记 8:20-21

巴别塔

全球洪水之后，上帝命令人生养众多，遍满全世界。那时候人类只说一种语言，只有一个政府，也有统一的文化。但因为人的罪性，他们趁这前所未有合一的机会，反叛创造他们的上帝。他们不愿分散各地，就在巴别（巴别位于今天的伊拉克境内）建

whole earth by confusing their languages. As people separated and spread out according to their languages, nations and ethnic groups began to form. The origins of all ethnic groups and nationalities, including the Chinese people, begins here.

"And God blessed Noah and his sons, and said unto them, Be fruitful, and multiply, and replenish the earth."　　　　Genesis 9:1

"And the whole earth was of one language and of one speech."
　　　　Genesis 11:1

"And they said, Go to, let us build us a city and a tower, whose top may reach unto heaven; and let us make us a name, lest we be scattered abroad upon the face of the whole earth."　　　　Genesis 11:4

"And the LORD said, Behold, the people is one, and they have all one language; and this they begin to do: and now nothing will be restrained from them, which they have imagined to do. Go to, let us go down, and there confound their language, that they may not understand one another's speech. So the LORD scattered them abroad from thence upon the face of all the earth: and they left off to build the city."
　　　　Genesis 11:6-8

King Yao 堯王

Yao was one of the great rulers from China's legendary period. He reigned before the founding of the Xia/Hsia 夏 Dynasty. Yao is best known for having passed on his rulership, not to his sons because he was *"insincere and quarrelsome."* [1] Yao gave it to a man named Shun 舜 who was virtuous and morally worthy to rule. King Yao once said: *"Point out someone among the illustrious, or set forth one from among the humble and mean."* So he searched and found a man named Shun, who was *"son of a blind man. His father was obstinately unprincipled; his step-mother was insincere; his half-brother Hsiang was arrogant. Yet, he has been able by his filial piety to live in harmony with them, and to lead them gradually to self-government, so that they no longer proceed to great wickedness."* [2]

King Shun 舜王

Shun lived from 2317 to 2208 B.C., and was the last king of China's legendary period. According to the *Shu Jing*, Yao offered Shun the throne after Shun proved his moral worthiness. Though Shun wished to decline in favor of someone more virtuous than himself, King Yao could find no such person. Upon ascending the throne, Shun offered sacrifices to Shang-Di 上帝 and to the

9

造一座能「通顶上天」的塔。因为他们的反叛，上帝将人的语言变乱，迫使他们分散各处。当人类分散，根据他们的语言遍布各地时，国家和种族就开始形成；所有种族和国家的起源，包括中华民族，就从那时开始了。

「上帝赐福给挪亚和他的儿子，对他们说：你们要生养众多，遍满了地。」　　　　　　　　　　创世记 9:1

「那时，天下人的口音，言语都是一样。」　创世记 11:1

「他们说：来吧！我们要建造一座城和一座塔，塔顶通天，为要传扬我们的名，免得我们分散全地上。」
　　　　　　　　　　　　　　　　　　　　创世记 11:4

「耶和华说：『看哪，他们成为一样的人民，都是一样的言语，如今既做起这事来，以后他们所要做的事就没有不成就的了。我们下去，在那里变乱他们的口音，使他们的言语彼此不通。』于是耶和华使他们从那里分散在全地上；他们就停工，不造那城了。」　创世记 11:6-8

尧

尧是中国传说时代最杰出的统治者之一，在夏朝之前治理中国。他以传贤不传子著称，因他的儿子「不真诚且常争闹」。[1] 尧传位给以品格和道德见称，配作统治者的舜。尧曾经指出：「选贤德不论出身贵贱」，所以他寻得了舜。舜的父亲是一个顽梗无德之人，继母诡诈，弟弟自大。然而舜却能守住孝道，与家人和睦相处，渐渐地善导他们，使他们不再步向劣途。[2]

舜

舜的年代是公元前 2317-2208 年，是中华文明传说时代最后一位统治者。《书经》记述，尧在考验舜的品格后，让位给舜。舜原本想拒绝，并希望尧能找到一位比自己更具德行的人选，但尧无法寻获比舜更好的人。在继位之时，舜在「堙」献祭与上帝

spirits 神 at the Round Mound.[3] This sacrifice to Shang-Di at the Round Mound is the same type of sacrifice that the Ming and Qing/Ching emperors offered to Shang-Di at the Temple/Altar of Heaven, located in present-day Beijing. We will discuss more about this sacrifice later. However it is important to note that at the very beginning of China's history Shun presents burnt offerings to Heaven on an altar specially prepared for that purpose.

King Yu 禹王

Yu, founder of the Xia/Hsia 夏 Dynasty, was appointed to the throne by Shun because of his ability to control China's great flood. He is the ruler credited with draining off the flood waters of the North China Plain. It is noteworthy that the founder of the Xia Dynasty, *"when his house was at its strength, he sought for able men to honor Shang-Di."* [4]

We see that the ancient Chinese believed that honoring Shang-Di was the most important factor for the empire to flourish. Up until the time of Shun virtue was the most important qualification for determining who was worthy enough to become the next ruler.   However, from the Xia Dynasty and onwards, heredity became the determining factor.

Xia/Hsia Dynasty 夏朝

Almost all we know about the Xia Dynasty originates from the *Shu Jing*. The Xia Dynasty lasted from 2070 to 1600 B.C.   Its decline marked the beginning of the Shang 商 Dynasty. It is noteworthy that throughout their entire history, the Chinese believed that it was ultimately an emperor's moral rectitude and good standing with the eternal God Shang-Di that qualified him for rulership.

Abraham (1996 - 1821 B.C.)

Before the Tower of Babel, all of humanity spoke only one language. Thus, when God revealed Himself, that revelation was passed to all peoples. After the dispersion at Babel, God no longer spoke directly to mankind as a whole. Instead, God chose Abraham (also known as Abram) to become the father of a new nation to receive His commandments and revelations. Abraham's descendants are known today as the Jewish people.   Once God had given the Jewish nation revelation concerning Himself, it was their responsibility to spread God's revelation to the rest of the world.   Abraham knew the one true God by the names *"El Shaddai"* and *"Jehovah."* The Hebrew "Jehovah" is translated as "LORD" in the English Bible, and "El Shaddai" is translated as "God Almighty."

及其它的神灵。³ 后来明清两朝君主在北京天坛上所主持的祭天之礼，与「堙」的祭礼是同一类型的，我们在后文会更多讨论这个祭祀。值得注意的是，在中国历史的初期，舜就在特别为上帝预备的祭坛献上燔祭。

禹

创立夏朝的禹，是因舜见他治理中国洪水有方，被立为王。他疏导了当时中国北方平原的洪水而为人称道。值得注意的是，「当夏王室强大的时候，他寻找有才德的人做官事，目的是敬事上帝。」⁴

所以我们从这里知道，中国人的祖先早已有了敬事上帝是最能令国家昌盛的概念。直到舜的时候，德行是决定君主资格的首要因素，但从夏朝起，世袭成为传承帝位的决定性因素。

夏朝

我们所知关有夏朝的资料几乎全来自《书经》。夏朝从公元前 2070 年到 1600 年。夏亡商继。这里值得我们注意的是，中国人相信，君主的兴亡至终都与他们的德行是否符合天理或违背天道有关。

亚伯拉罕（公元前 1996 – 1821 年）

在建造巴别塔以前，世人只说一种语言；因此当上帝向世人启示的时候，祂的启示传向全人类。但当世人在巴别塔被上帝分散各地之后，上帝不再直接向全人类启示。他拣选了亚伯兰（后来改名为亚伯拉罕）去成为一国的国父，来接受祂的吩咐和启示。亚伯拉罕的后代就是今天的犹太人。上帝特选犹太族，给他们责任把祂的启示传给全世人。亚伯拉罕称这位唯一的真神为「全能神」（El Shaddai）和「耶和华」（Jehovah）。希伯来文的耶和华（Jehovah）在英文圣经里是大写的「主」（LORD），而 El Shaddai 则翻译为「全能的上帝」。

"Now the LORD had said unto Abram, Get thee out of thy country, and from thy kindred, and from thy father's house, unto a land that I will shew thee: And I will make of thee a great nation, and I will bless thee, and make thy name great; and thou shalt be a blessing: And I will bless them that bless thee, and curse him that curseth thee: and in thee shall all families of the earth be blessed."   Genesis 12:1-3

Melchizedek

Melchizedek was the Canaanite king and priest of Salem (later known as Jerusalem) during the time of Abram. Melchizedek personally knew the one true supreme God by the name *"El Elyon"*, translated in the English Bible as *"God Most High."* After Abram fought and defeated several kings in battle, he returned to Canaan and encountered Melchizedek. After receiving a blessing from Melchizedek, Abram identified *"El Elyon"* of the Canaanites as being the same God as *"Jehovah."*

"And Melchizedek king of Salem brought forth bread and wine: and he was the priest of the most high God [Hebrew: El Elyon]. And he (Melchizedek) blessed him (Abram), and said, Blessed be Abram of the most high God [El Elyon], possessor of heaven and earth."

Genesis 14:18-19

"But Abram said to the king of Sodom, I have lift up my hand to the LORD [Hebrew: Jehovah], the most high God [El Elyon], the possessor of heaven and earth."   Genesis 14:22

We see that the God of the Bible has revealed Himself to different peoples and nations by different names but always with the same basic meaning ("most high God" and "most powerful God', i.e. Creator God). Abraham, a Hebrew, knew the one true God by the name *"Jehovah"* while Melchizedek knew Him as *"El Elyon."* This same creator God has revealed Himself to the Chinese people by the name Shang-Di 上帝 and Heaven 天! The God of the Bible did NOT ignore the Chinese for 5,000 years of their history! He has always been there from the very beginning! Continue reading to find out more about this exciting history!

Jacob/Israel

Jacob (also called Israel) was the grandson of Abraham and forefather of the Jewish people. His twelve sons became the twelve tribes of the nation Israel.

13

「耶和华对亚伯兰说：你要离开本地，本族，父家，往我所要指示你的地去。我必叫你成为大国。我必赐福给你，叫你的名为大，你也要叫别人得福。为你祝福的，我必赐福给他；咒诅你的，我必咒诅他。地上的万族都要因你得福。」 创世记 12:1-3

麦基洗德

麦基洗德在亚伯拉罕那时代是撒冷城（后改名为耶路撒冷）的王和祭司。他所认识和敬拜的那位真神名为 El Elyon，翻译为「至高神」。圣经记载，当亚伯拉罕在战场上击败几位王之后，他回到迦南遇见麦基洗德。麦基洗德为亚伯拉罕祝福，而亚伯拉罕认知迦南人麦基洗德所拜的「至高神」，就是他所敬拜的「耶和华」。

「又有撒冷王麦基洗德带着饼和酒出来迎接，他(麦基洗德)是至高神的祭司。他为亚伯兰祝福，说：愿天地的主，至高的神赐福与亚伯兰。」 创世记 14:18-19

「亚伯兰对所多玛王说：我已经向天地的主，至高的神耶和华起誓。」 创世记 14:22

由此可见，《圣经》里的上帝向不同的民族和国家，用不同的名字启示自己，但这些名字均有基本同样的意义（「至高的」，「全能的」，即造物主）。希伯来人亚伯拉罕称那位唯一的真神为「耶和华」，而迦南人麦基洗德称这位唯一的真神为「至高神」。而这位创造万物的主，中国人称祂为「上帝」和「天」！《圣经》中的上帝没有在中国人五千年的历史中忘了他们，祂在起初就存在他们的历史中！请你继续读下去，来明白这个精彩的历史！

雅各/以色列

雅各（后来称以色列）是亚伯拉罕的孙子，犹太人的先祖；他的十二个儿子后来成为以色列国的十二支派。

Nation of Israel Enters Egypt

Jacob (Israel) and his entire family left their homeland because of severe famine, and enter Egypt approximately 1706 B.C. At first everything went well but after many years the Egyptians enslaved the Jews.

Moses

About 400 years after God promised to make Abraham a great nation, He freed Abraham's descendants from slavery in Egypt (Gen. 15:13-16). Moses was the man God had called to free the Jewish nation. This great deliverance began with Moses' vision of the Burning Bush. There, God revealed Himself for the first time by His name *"I AM"*.

> *"And God said to Moses, I AM THAT I AM. And He said, Thus shalt thou say unto the children of Israel, I AM [Hebrew: Yahweh = "I AM"] has sent me to you."*   Exodus 3:14

Old Testament Prophecies Concerning Messiah

From approximately 1400 B.C. to 400 B.C. prophecies concerning the Messiah were recorded in the Old Testament of the Bible. The Messiah is the one whom God promised that He would send to save and free humanity from the penalty and power of sin.

Shang / Yin Dynasty 商/殷朝

This dynasty ruled from 1765 to 1122 B.C. All of the Shang kings mentioned in the *Shu Jing* have been verified by the Shang oracle bones. [5]

The Supreme God of the Shang people was Shang-Di 上帝. He was the omnipotent Supreme God at the top of the spiritual hierarchy who had control over the rain, harvests, and victories or defeats in battle. At this point in history, we have the oldest existing writing of Chinese characters, which are found in the Shang oracle bones.

The oracle bones were usually turtle shells or cow bones engraved with Chinese characters, many of which are still preserved to the present day. We find that Shang-Di was already an all-powerful, all-knowing Supreme Deity in China's earliest beginnings. He was already present in His full glory as the Supreme God above all else.

以色列进入埃及

在大约公元前 1706 年，雅各（以色列）以及全家因为饥荒，离开家乡迁移到埃及。起初一切都还安好，但经过多年后，埃及人开始奴役犹太人。

摩西

约在公元前 1450 年，上帝呼召摩西去解救在埃及被法老王奴役的犹太人。祂在荆棘火中向摩西显现，将此任务交给摩西，而且就在那时刻，头一次将祂的名字是「自有永有」的意义显示出来。

「上帝对摩西说：我是自有永有的。又说：你要对以色列人这样说：那自有永有的打发我到你们这里来。」

出埃及记 3:14

《圣经》中旧约经文对救世主弥赛亚的预言

从公元前 1400 年至 400 年，《旧约圣经》记录了有关弥赛亚的许多预言。上帝应许世人，祂会派遣一位救世主把世人从罪的刑罚和权势中拯救出来。

商朝/殷朝

商朝从公元前 1765 到 1122 年。《书经》中所提及商朝的君王，都得到了出土的甲骨文的证实。[5]

商朝人最至高无上的神是上帝，祂是全能的神，掌管雨水，收成，和战争的胜负。存到今天的商朝甲骨文，是中国最早的文字记录。

甲骨文通常是刻在龟骨或牛骨上的字样，许多一直被保存到现今。我们从甲骨文知道，在中国最早期，先祖已认识到上帝是无所不能、无所不知的至高神；祂已经以最荣耀，且超越一切之上的身份存在。

Above is a sample Shang oracle bone. Thousands have been discovered by archaeologists

Wu Yi 武乙

Emperor Wu Yi, who reigned for only four short years, was considered to be one of the most corrupt Shang Dynasty rulers. For over a thousand years of early Chinese history, there was no known record of the Chinese ever fashioning idol images. Wu Yi is attributed with making the first idol image in Chinese history. According to Sima Qian 司馬遷, the Grand Historian of the Han, Wu Yi made an idol of Shang-Di from wood. Then, he played dice with it, causing someone else to play on behalf of the image. When the idol of Shang-Di lost the game, Wu Yi would ridicule and disgrace the image. He would then make a leather bag filled with pig blood, hang it on the idol's neck, and shoot it with an arrow, causing blood to splatter everywhere. He called this sport "shooting at Heaven 射天." In the fourth year of his reign, while hunting between the Ho and Wei Rivers, he was suddenly struck dead by lightning from heaven.

The people recognized this as the appropriate vengeance of Heaven, whom Wu Yi had insulted. [6] The Chinese knew that they were never to make an idol of Shang-Di, and they almost never did throughout their 5,000 years of history.

Zhou/Chou Dynasty 周朝

The Zhou Dynasty began in 1121 B.C. with King Wu's 武王 conquest of the Shang people, and lasted until 249 B.C. At this time in their history, we are told *"great importance was attached to teaching the people about sacrifice."* [7] The *Shu Jing* explains that the Shang people were defeated because they did not live up to the virtuous standards. The Zhou tribe knew the one true God by the name Tian 天, or Heaven, who had supreme power over the universe and humanity. In their own writings, they regarded Heaven and Shang-Di to be the same deity – two

17

图示考古学家在上一世纪
发掘出商朝其中之一的甲骨文

武乙

武乙虽然在位只有四年，却是商朝最残暴的统治者之一。在中国最早期的一千多年里，没有任何记录表明中国人的先祖造过任何偶像，武乙是第一个。根据汉朝历史学家司马迁的记载，武乙用木头造偶像，并命名那木偶为天神。然后他让人代表偶像，跟他玩掷骰子游戏。当对方掷输了，武乙便奚落、羞辱那木像。武乙又用盛满猪血的皮袋挂在木像的颈上，用箭射破皮袋，以至血花四溅，武乙称这为「射天」。武乙在位的第四年于打猎途中突然被雷电击中而亡。

百姓都认定这是武乙凌辱上帝的报应。[6] 在中国五千年的历史中，罕有一个中国人敢妄做上帝的雕像。

周朝

周朝始于公元前 1121 年，自武王攻克商开始，直至公元前 249 年。此期「教民祭祀是件大事」。[7] 根据《书经》所载，商之所以败亡乃因道德衰微。周人认识掌管宇宙万物唯一的真神，

names for the same Supreme God. The Zhou argued that it was useless for the Shang to resist because Heaven willed that the House of Zhou should rule. This doctrine came to be known as Tian Ming 天命, or Heaven's Mandate, and it formed the cornerstone of the Chinese state. Heaven, they said, elected or commanded certain men to be rulers over the tribes of the world, and their heirs continued to exercise this power as long as they carried out their religious and administrative duties with piety, wisdom, and justice.

They knew that if they turned their backs on Shang-Di and the spirits, and abandoned the virtuous ways that had made them worthy to rule, then Heaven would discard them and elect a new family or tribe to rule. The Shang kings, they argues, had once been wise and benevolent rulers, and thus enjoyed the full blessing and sanction of Heaven. But in later years, they had become cruel and degenerate. Thus, Heaven called upon the Zhou chieftains to overthrow and punish the Shang to usher in a new dynasty.

Sometime during the early Zhou period, the Zhou rulers also introduced the concept that the emperor was the Son of Heaven 天子. Thus, they argued that the emperor, being the Son of Heaven, was the only one worthy enough to worship Shang-Di. Shang-Di, after all, was too high for the common people to worship. As a result, the common people were forbidden to worship Shang-Di. From that time onward, only the emperor would worship Shang-Di, usually once a year on the winter solstice (around December 22nd), and a few other rare occasions. At this point in history, the common people began to lose touch and forget Shang-Di. Most modern scholars believe that the motivation for these new teachings was for the Zhou to consolidate political power.

Buddha

Buddha, also known as Siddhartha Gautama, was the founder of Buddhism. He lived from 557 B.C. to 477 B.C. in India. He never claimed to be a deity or divinely inspired.

Laozi/Lao Tzu 老子

Laozi was the founder of Taoism and was born in 604 BC. He taught that rather than strive for success, men should pursue a passive inaction, and that all things will come naturally to a successful conclusion. Taoism is not the true spiritual roots of the Chinese people. It was introduced over 1,500 years after the beginning of Chinese civilization.

称祂为「天」。根据周人的文献，上帝跟「天」是同一位神，只是两个不同的称谓。周人相信朝代的更迭乃出于天命，这「天命论」也成了后世历代皇朝更替的基本要道。「天命论」指出：上天会派选某些人去统治国家，只要他们的子孙持续以敬虔、智慧、和正义施政，他们就有承继这权力的资格。

他们也知道，一旦背弃了上帝和神明，以及使他们配当统治者的德行，那么上天会丢弃他们，去选择一新的家族或部落来统治。他们声称，商朝的君主曾是有智慧和仁慈的统治者，所以得到上天的祝佑和称许；但在商末，统治者变得残酷腐败，因此上天派遣周的领袖去推翻并惩罚商，建立一个新的朝代。

在周的早期，统治者开始传递皇帝是「天子」的概念，并声称只有身为天子的皇帝，才配得敬拜上帝，普通老百姓没有资格去敬拜这位高高在上的上帝。结果是，普通老百姓被禁止去敬拜上帝。从那时开始，只有君王在冬至（约在 12 月 22 日）及一些特别的时令去敬拜上帝，而普通百姓则渐而远离且忘记上帝了。多数现代学者相信，周王使用这新的政策来巩固自身的政权。

释迦牟尼

释迦牟尼创立了佛教。他在公元前 557 年生于印度，死于公元前 477 年。释迦牟尼从来没有自称为神，或有来自神的启示。

老子

老子是道家的始祖，生于公元前 604 年。他不教导人努力去追求成功，反而传播「无为」的道理，以静制动，万事顺其自然，就必有成果。道教并不是中国人初始的灵性根源，它在中华文明开启后大约 1500 年才出现。

Confucius 孔夫子

Confucius lived from 551 BC to 479 BC in the Shandong 山東 Province. He is considered to be China's greatest sage, philosopher, and educator. Confucius lived in a period when the Zhou Empire was in its decline, and the provinces were fighting for supremacy. During his lifetime, he attempted to restore the glory of the Zhou Empire by reviving the moral values of the ancient past. Confucius looked to the golden ages of the sage-emperors Yao 堯, Shun 舜, and the early kings of the Zhou Dynasty who ruled the empire with virtue and wisdom, when all was at peace. He revised and compiled several books now contained in the *Chinese Classics* 四書五經, including the *Book of History* 書經, the *Book of Poetry* 詩經, and *Spring and Autumn Annals* 春秋. Though Confucius himself never claimed to be a god, Confucian temples are found throughout China and Taiwan today where many Chinese worship him. Though he was a great teacher and philosopher, our true spiritual roots as Chinese are not found through worshipping Confucius.

Mencius 孟子

Mencius was a follower of Confucian thought, and lived from 371 to 289 BC. He helped develop Confucianism.

Warring States Period 戰國

The Warring States period, spanning from 453 B.C. to 221 B.C., was a time of great political, social, religious, and cultural chaos. Disunity within the Zhou Empire eventually led to civil war where each province fought for supremacy. During this period, much of the rites and music associated with the worship of Shang-Di 上帝 became corrupt amid the contending states.[8] These rituals finally perished after the State of Qin 秦 emerged as the final victor of the Warring States Period. It wasn't until the Ming Dynasty that many of these rituals associated with the worship of Shang-Di were restored and established once again.[9]

Qin/Chin Empire 秦朝

In 221 B.C., after more than 200 years of constant warfare, the State of Qin/Chin emerges as the final victor, unifying China and putting an end to the Warring States Period. Upon his conquest, the king of Qin assumed the title "First Emperor of Qin" 秦始皇帝. It is from "Chin" 秦 where the terms "China" and "Chinese" are derived. The First Emperor standardized the writing system, currency, weights, and measures. In 213 B.C., he issued the infamous order to "Burn the Books" on the advice of his prime minister, Li Si 李斯. Then, in 212

孔夫子

孔夫子是山东人，公元前 551 年至公元前 479 年，被誉为中国最伟大的圣贤、哲学家和教育家。他生于周朝皇权式微，诸侯奋起的战乱时代，一生致力于复兴周朝的光荣，以及重返先前的道德价值。他景仰圣贤的尧、舜和周朝早期统治者「以德治国，天下太平」的黄金时代。他集成了「四书五经」中的几部经典作品，包括《书经》、《诗经》和《春秋》。虽然孔夫子从来没有自称为神，后人却于中国大陆及台湾各地建立庙宇去祭拜他。孔子虽然是一位伟大的教育家和哲学家，但祭祀孔子不是中国人灵性信仰的根源。

孟子

孟子是跟随孔子思想的一位哲学家，生于公元前 371 年，死于公元前 289 年，他帮助了儒家学说的发扬。

战国时代

战国时代约由公元前 453 年到公元前 221 年，是政治、社会、宗教和文化都至为纷乱的时期。周王朝本身的分裂，加上各诸侯互相争霸，导致敬拜上帝的礼和乐在各地都败坏了。[8]到了秦统一各国，结束战国时，所有祭仪全然失传。一直到明朝，许多祭祀上帝的礼仪才重新恢复建立起来。

秦朝

经过两百多年的战乱，公元前 221 年，秦的君主统一中国，结束了战国时代。秦王登基后自立为始皇帝，「中国」和「中国人」的名称就来自于「秦 Chin」。始皇帝统一文字、货币及度量衡。公元前 213 年，秦始皇听从宰相李斯的建议，颁布「焚书」，公元前 212 年，下令「坑儒」。秦始皇又建

B.C., he ordered Confucian scholars to be buried alive. He also erected four altars to offer sacrifices to the White, Green Yellow, and Red Di's 帝. Later, after Liu Bang 劉邦 overthrew the Qin Empire, he founded the Han Dynasty and adopted the same erroneous practice of sacrificing to the four Di's, and even invented the Black Di. It is noteworthy that we find absolutely nothing concerning these five false Di's in the *Book of History* 書經.

Above is the Chinese Terracotta Army located at the tomb of the First Emperor of Qin. It was accidentally discovered in March 1974 and is now renowned as the 8th Wonder of the World. It consists of more than 7,000 life-sized figures of warriors and horses buried with Qin.

It was under Emperor Wu 漢武帝, that the sacrifice to Shang-Di was altogether neglected. Later scholars and philosophers had difficulty comprehending the worship of these false Di's. They argued that there was only one Heaven. How then could there be five Di's? As a result, they introduced the idea that there were six heavens, where the five Di's and Shang-Di lived. The worship of these five false Di's and the six heavens continued until the time of the Ming Dynasty. The Ming abolished the worship of these five false Di's and re-established the true worship of Shang-Di as the one Supreme God above all else. [10]

Burning of the Books

In 213 B.C., the First Emperor, who abhorred Confucian philosophy, issued the infamous order to "Burn the Books" on the advice of his prime minister Li Si

四座坛拜白、青、黄、赤四帝。及至汉高祖刘邦推翻秦建立汉朝，他不但承袭了对白、青、黄、赤四帝错误的祭祀，更自创一个黑帝来拜。值得注意的是，《书经》里面根本找不到有关这五个帝的文字记录。

在 1974 年意外发现秦始皇坟墓的兵马俑。现在
已列为世界第八奇观。它有超过七千真人大小的
兵和马埋在秦始皇墓内。

汉武帝时，皇族遗弃了对上帝的敬拜。后来学者们和哲学家们无法了解祭祀五帝的概念，他们争辩只有一个天，如何有五个帝呢？结果他们发明了「六天」的说法，说那是五帝和上帝居住的地方。「五帝六天」的祭拜持续到明朝。明朝废除五帝的敬拜，重新恢复对至高上帝的真实祭拜。[9]

焚书

公元前 213 年，始皇帝因憎恨儒家学说，听从了宰相李斯的建议，实行焚书，「四书五经」险而失传。这些经书蒙上帝眷佑被保存到今天，让我们可以考究有关中国人敬拜上帝的始李斯. It was because of this event that we almost lost the *Chinese Classics* 四書五經. We are very fortunate today that these books were preserved to the present day by the providence of God. We would not be able to present the exciting message contained in this booklet had the *Chinese Classics* been lost in the fires of Qin.

Buddhism Enters China from India

Buddhism enters China around 67 B.C. from India. Buddhism is a religion of Indian invention. It is not of Chinese origin, and therefore cannot contain the true spiritual roots of the Chinese people.

Plato & Aristotle

Plato lived from 427 B.C. to 347 B.C., and Aristotle lived from 384 B.C. to 322 B.C. They are considered to be among the greatest philosophers of the Greek world. In their writings, they refer to the one true God as *"Theos"* and *"Logos."* The early Christians of the first century A.D. realized that this was the name by which God had revealed himself to the Greeks. Thus they adopted these terms as legitimate names for the one true God. In fact, the New Testament was originally written in Greek, and uses the terms *"Theos"* and *"Logos"* as the name for the one true God of creation. The Greek *"Logos"* is translated as "Word" (with a capital W) in the English Bible (John 1:1, 14), and *"Theos"* is translated as "God."

> *"In the beginning was the Word [Greek: Logos = "Word"], and the Word [Logos] was with God [Greek: Theos = "God"], and the Word [Logos] was God [Theos]."* John 1:1

Jesus Christ Comes to Earth

From the Bible we learn that Jesus Christ is the promised Messiah: the Savior that God promised to send to save mankind from the penalty and power of sin. Though he himself was sinless, Jesus Christ suffered and died on the cross for our sins because the penalty for sin is death. God is both a God of love and justice. Therefore, He must execute justice by punishing sin. Jesus took those penalties upon Himself so that we might not have to pay it ourselves. Being sinless He resurrected from the dead the third day, and ascended back to heaven never to die again.

源，真可算是幸运的。若「四书五经」真丧失于秦火中，今日我们就不能与您分享这小册子里精彩的信息了。

佛教自印度传入中国

佛教在公元前 67 年从印度传入中国。佛教源于印度，不是中国人原有的信仰，更不是中国人灵性的根源。

柏拉图与亚里士多德

柏拉图生活在公元前 427 至 347 年，亚里士多德生活在公元前 384 至 322 年；他们被誉为古希腊最伟大的哲学家。在他们的著作中，他们使用希腊文字「Theos」和「Logos」来称呼唯一的真神。第一世纪的基督徒知道这名称是上帝向希腊人的启示，所以他们采用这希腊文字为唯一真神的名字。事实上，用希腊文写作的《新约圣经》就是用「Theos」和「Logos」这两字称唯一创造天地的真神。希腊人的「Logos」在《圣经》被译作「道」（约翰福音 1：1，14），「Theos」被译作「上帝」。

「太初有道（道＝Logos），道与上帝（上帝＝Theos）同在，道就是上帝。」　　　　　　　　约翰福音 1:1

耶稣基督降世

耶稣基督就是《圣经》上所预言上帝应许人类、拯救他们脱离罪恶和死亡的救世主，又称弥赛亚。《圣经》记述，耶稣是无罪的，但祂却为我们承担一切的罪死在十字架上，因为罪的代价是死亡。上帝是爱与正义的真神，祂必须惩罚罪恶来实行正义，所以耶稣代

The Bible, God's Word, teaches us that if we repent of our sins, trust in Christ alone for our salvation, and receive Him as our Lord and Savior into our hearts, we shall be saved from the condemnation of sin and final judgment. He alone can save us from the eternal torments of hell.

"In the beginning was the Word, and the Word was with God, and the Word was God. The same was in the beginning with God...He was in the world, and the world was made by Him, and the world knew Him not... And the Word was made flesh and dwelt among us (and we beheld His glory, the glory as of the only begotten of the Father), full of grace and truth."   John 1:1,10,14

"For all have sinned and fall short of the glory of God."   Romans 3:23

"For the wages of sin is death; but the gift of God is eternal life through Jesus Christ our Lord."   Romans 6:23

"That if thou shalt confess with thy mouth the Lord Jesus, and shalt believe in thine heart that God has raised Him from the dead, thou shalt be saved."   Romans 10:9

"And Jesus said unto her, I am the resurrection and the life. He who believes in me, though he may die, he shall live. And whoever lives and believes in me shall never die..."   John 11:25

"For God so loved the world, that He gave is only begotten Son, that whosoever believes in Him should not perish, but have everlasting life."   John 3:16

Ming Dynasty 明朝

The Ming Dynasty lasted from 1368 to 1644 A.D. From the Han 漢 Dynasty until the end of the Yuan 元 Dynasty, the emperors of China continued the corrupt practice of sacrificing to the five Di's and six Heavens. However, the Ming desired to return to their true spiritual roots. So they appointed two committees at the beginning of their dynasty to investigate topics pertaining to the corruption of the rites and music. After they had completed their research, the Ming family abolished the sacrifices to the six heavens and to the five Di's. These sacrifices, they maintained, had been added to the original rituals performed by the Xia, Shang, and early Zhou, which knew of only two great border sacrifices -- those to Heaven and earth. It was the Ming who researched their ancient beliefs and restored the emperor's worship of Shang-Di, as close as they could, to its original form under the Xia, Shang, and early Zhou emperors. Based on their research, they then built the Temple/Altar of Heaven for the worship of Shang-Di (i.e. Heaven) and attempted to re-establish the rituals and music as close to its original form as possible. We can learn a lot about what the ancient Chinese believed by Shang-Di by examining these rituals.

27

替我们担负了惩罚。无罪的耶稣三日后从死里复活，返回天堂永不再死。《圣经》告诉我们，如果我们悔改自己的罪，从心里接受耶稣基督为救主和生命的主，我们就必从自己的过犯和罪的惩罚中得救，死后也不会受地狱永死的刑罚。

> 「太初有道，道与上帝同在，道就是上帝。这道太初与上帝同在……祂在世界，世界也是藉着祂造的，世界却不认识祂……道成了肉身，住在我们中间，充充满满地有恩典有真理。我们也见过祂的荣光，正是父独生子的荣光。」　　　　　约翰福音 1:1-2, 10, 14

> 「因为世人都犯了罪，亏缺了上帝的荣耀。」
> 　　　　　　　　　　　　　　　　罗马书 3:23

> 「因为罪的工价乃是死；惟有上帝的恩赐，在我们的主基督耶稣里，乃是永生。」　　　　　罗马书 6:23

> 「你若口里认耶稣为主，心里信上帝叫祂从死里复活，就必得救。」　　　　　　　　　罗马书 10:9

> 「耶稣对她说：复活在我，生命也在我。信我的人虽然死了，也必复活。凡活着信我的人必永远不死。你信这话吗？」　　　　　　　　　约翰福音 11:25-26

> 「上帝爱世人，甚至将祂的独生子赐给他们，叫一切信祂的，不致灭亡，反得永生。」　　约翰福音 3:16

明朝

明朝自公元后 1368 至 1644 年。自汉至元，中国的君主奉行祭祀「五帝六天」腐败的礼仪。然而，明朝愿回归他们真正灵性的根本，所以在开朝之初就派任两组人员，调查有关祭礼与祭乐如何腐败的沿革。在完成考察后，明朝废除「五帝六天」的拜祭。他们的理由是，这些祭祀是夏、商、周早期原本仅有对天、地的郊祀之外增添的。明朝考察了他们古老的信仰，恢复对上帝的敬拜，尽其可能地贴近原本夏、商、周早期的形式。他们更依据考察的结果，建筑天坛去敬拜上帝（天），且尽可能使用最接近原本的祭礼与祭乐。[10] 从他们的祭仪中，我们可以学到很多上古中国人对上帝的信仰与观念。

Temple/Altar of Heaven 天壇 Built

Located in southeast Beijing stands the monument called "Tian Tan" 天壇, built specifically for the emperor's worship of Shang-Di.

Hall of Prayer for Good Harvests

Danbi Bridge

Butcher Pavilion

Imperial Vault of Heaven

Gate of Hell (Beneath Danbi Bridge

Fasting Palace (not shown here)

Circular Mound Altar

Aerial Photograph of the Temple/Altar of Heaven complex, with its main structures labeled.

天坛的建筑

天坛位于北京城的东南方，是特别为皇帝祭祀上帝而造的。

祈年殿

宰牲亭

丹陛桥

鬼门关

皇穹宇

斋宫
（不在图）

圆丘坛

鸟瞰天坛的各主要建筑物

Although in English we know this monument as the "Temple of Heaven," the word "tan" (altar = 壇) means "altar," not "temple" (temple = 廟). Therefore, we can more accurately refer to it as the "Altar of Heaven." This monument consists of several distinct structures that can be seen in the accompanying aerial photograph.

Notice the Circular Mound Altar 圜丘壇, Fasting Palace 齋宮, Danbi Bridge 丹陛橋, Hall of Prayer for Good Harvests 祈年殿, Imperial Vault of Heaven 皇穹宇, and Butcher Pavilion 宰牲亭. Among all the sights and wonders in China, only the Great Wall rivals the Temple of Heaven in popularity as a tourist attraction.

After its completion in 1420 A.D., the Altar of Heaven was repaired and expanded many times in the following 300 years. The two main builders were Emperor Jia Jing 嘉靖 and Emperor Qian Long 乾隆. It was here that the emperors of the Ming and Qing dynasties offered sacrifices to worship Shang-Di once a year on the winter solstice in December.

So important was this sacrifice that Confucius himself, when asked about the meaning of the "great sacrifice" 大祭, replied: *"I do not know. He who knew its meaning would find it as easy to govern the kingdom as to look on this; -- 'pointing to his palm.'"* [11] We see that the true spiritual meaning of these sacrifices to Shang-Di had already been lost by the time of Confucius. The rituals remained in tact, but its true spiritual meaning was lost.

The good news is that because Shang-Di is also the same God of Christianity, we can re-discover the meaning of these Heaven-worshipping rituals by comparing them with the revelation within the Bible!

The annual Heaven-worshipping ceremony began at the Hanqiu Tan 圜丘壇, or Circular Mound Altar. The origin of this altar extends at least as far back as the time of Shun 舜, who offered sacrifices to Shang-Di at the Round Mound upon ascending the throne.

The Ming established this Round Mound into the Circular Mound Altar for offering sacrifices to Shang-Di. Every year on the winter solstice the emperor would come in person to this particular altar to pray and present sacrifices to Shang-Di. The sacrifice usually consisted of a *"calf-bull, of unmixed [one solid] color and without flaw."* [12] It as here that the emperor thanked Heaven for the year's good harvest and the country's prosperity, and asked Shang-Di to grant prosperity and peace for the coming year.

But why was the sacrifice supposed to be of unmixed color and without flaw? And why must it be offered upon an altar?

虽然我们称这所建筑群为"Temple of Heaven"（天庙），它实际上是一座「坛」(altar)，而非「庙」(temple)，所以对它正确的称呼应是"Altar of Heaven"（天坛）。这座建筑群包括几个主要的结构，请看上页鸟瞰图。

天坛建筑群中有圜丘坛、斋宫、皇穹宇、丹陛桥、宰牲亭、祈年殿等。在中国所有观光胜地中，只有长城的地位能够与天坛并驾齐驱。

自公元 1420 年建成后，天坛在往后的三百年中经过了无数次修复与扩建，明朝嘉靖和清朝乾隆两皇帝是主要的兴建者。明清两朝的君王每年在十二月冬至时，在天坛献上祭物来祭拜上帝。

这个祭祀是如此重要，甚至孔子在被问及「大祭」的意义时，他回答说：「不知也，知其说者，之于天下也，其如示诸斯乎，指其掌。」[11]

孔子的意思就是说：「我不知道。如果有人知道，治天下就好比伸手看掌那么容易了。」可见祭祀上帝的意义，早在孔子时代已失传；祭礼的形式虽在，但其意义已失传。然由于皇天上帝与基督教的上帝是同一位，拿祭天的礼仪与《圣经》内相关的记述相比较，我们可以重新找到祭天礼仪的真正意义。

每年皇帝对天的祭祀大典从圜丘坛开始。这种在祭坛献祭的仪式可以追溯到舜王时代。舜王在继位之初，即在圜丘（土坛）献牲敬拜上帝。

明朝将圜丘扩大，来向上帝献祭。皇帝在每年冬至，亲自来到圜丘坛向上帝祷告并献上祭物。祭物通常包括「无杂色，完美无瑕的公牛。」[12]皇帝在此感谢上苍赐下本年的丰收与国家昌盛，并祈祷来年的昌盛与平安。

但是为什么祭物必须是无杂色，且完美无瑕的呢？为什么一定要献在坛上呢？

The Circular Mound Altar

*"Then Noah builded an **altar** unto the LORD, and took of every clean beast, and of every clean fowl, and **offered burnt offerings on the altar**. And the LORD smelled a sweet savor..."*   Genesis 8:20-21

*"If any man of you bring an offering unto the LORD, ye shall bring your offering of the **cattle**, even of the herd, and of the flock. If his offering be a **burnt sacrifice** of the herd, let him offer a male **without blemish**...and he shall put his hand upon the head of the burnt offering, and it shall be accepted for him to make atonement for him"*   Leviticus 1:2-4

*"And he said unto Aaron, 'Take thee a young calf for a sin offering, and a ram for **a burnt offering, without blemish**, and offer them before the LORD."*   Leviticus 9:2

We see here that the historical account found in the Holy Bible agrees amazingly well with the account found in Chinese history! In fact, even the Chinese word for sacrifice 犧 bears witness to this truth.

$$牛 \;+\; 羊 \;+\; 秀 \;+\; 戈 \;=\; 犧$$

bull, ox   lamb   beautiful   spear head   sacrifice
(unblemished)

These practices of offering burnt sacrifices began with Noah's sacrifice to the God of Heaven upon exiting the ark after the Flood. The Bible clearly states that the sacrificial animals used in the burnt sacrifices symbolize Jesus Christ. The sacrifice was usually either a lamb or an ox, and must be without flaw or blemish to symbolize Jesus' perfection and sinless life.

*"The next day John seeth Jesus coming unto him, and saith, 'Behold, the **Lamb of God** which taketh away the sin of the world!'"*   John 1:29

33

圜丘坛图示
The Circular Mound Altar

「挪亚为耶和华筑了一座坛，拿各类洁净的牲畜，飞鸟献在坛上为燔祭，耶和华闻那馨香之气……」
创世记 8:20-21

「你们中间若有人献供物给耶和华，要从牛群羊群中，献牲畜为供物。他的供物若以牛为燔祭，就要在会幕门口献一只没有残疾的公牛，可以在耶和华面前蒙悦纳。他要按手在燔祭牲的头上，燔祭便蒙悦纳，为他赎罪。」
利未记 1:2-4

「对亚伦说：你当取牛群中的一只公牛较为赎罪祭，一只公绵羊作燔祭，都要没有残疾的，献在耶和华面前。」
利未记 9:2

我们在此看见，圣经的历史记录奇妙地与中国历史的记载相吻合！事实上，甚至中国的「犠」这个字都见证了这个真理。

牛 + 羊 + 秀 + 戈 = 犠（牺）

这样的祭礼可追溯至挪亚在洪水退去后，出方舟献祭给天上的真神。《圣经》清楚明说在献燔祭时所用的牺牲象征着主耶稣基督，它们通常都是羔羊或公牛，而且一定要是完美无瑕疵的，用以象征耶稣完美、无罪的一生。

「次日，约翰看见耶稣来到他那儿，就说：看哪，上帝的羔羊，除去世人罪孽的！」
约翰福音 1:29

A close up view of the Danbi Bridge

The Gate of Hell:
an arched gateway
beneath Danbi Bridge

The sacrificial animals the emperor presented to Shang-Di at the Circular Mound Altar were sent to the Butcher Pavilion 宰牲亭 through an arched gateway called the Gate of Hell 鬼門關. Originally called the "gate allowing cattle" 走牲道, it is located beneath the Danbi Bridge 丹陛橋. It became known as the Gate of Hell because all animals that went through it must die. None of the sacrificial animals were allowed to walk on the Danbi Bridge. Perhaps the Chinese had some understanding that these sacrificial animals symbolically took the penalty for their sin.

According to the Bible, Jesus Christ was the sinless sacrifice who took the penalty of our sins by suffering and dying a horrible death on the cross. On the third day, he rose from the dead never to die again! If we believe in Him, we shall be saved from the gates of Hell!

"But God commendeth his love toward us, in that, while we were yet sinners, Christ died for us. Much more then, being now justified by his blood, we shall be saved from wrath through him." Romans 5:8-9

35

近观丹陛桥

丹陛桥下的鬼门关

皇帝用来献祭的牲畜被牵过鬼门关，带到宰牲亭。这道门本叫「走牲道」，位于丹陛桥底下，后来被称为鬼门关，是因为从这走过的动物注定是要被宰杀的。没有一只备祭的动物可以走在丹陛桥上面。也许古代中国人明白备祭的动物是为我们代罪的象征。

《圣经》也说无罪的耶稣基督代替我们的罪被钉死于十字架上，第三天从死里复活，永不再死！倘若我们相信祂，我们就免于鬼门关的死亡。

「惟有基督在我们还作罪人的时候为我们死，在此向我们显明了。现在我们既靠著他的血称义，就神的爱就更要藉著他免去神的忿怒。」　　　　　罗马书 5：8-9

The Zhai Gong 齋宫, or Fasting Palace, was located near the West Gate. This is where the emperor fasted for three days before he was allowed to worship Heaven. In addition to fasting, he also abstained from recreation, women, and handling of criminal cases. The emperor must demonstrate his humility and pure heart toward Shang-Di before he can worship him. Shang-Di would accept nothing less than the emperor's whole heart, mind, and soul.

Front Entrance to the Fasting Palace. This is where the emperor fasted for three days before worshipping Heaven.

Confucius said, "He who offends against Heaven has none to whom he can pray." [13]

"If I regard iniquity in my heart, the Lord will not hear me."
Psalms 66:18

"Blessed are the pure in heart: for they shall see God."   Matthew 5:8

"Thou shalt love the LORD thy God with all thy heart, with all thy soul, with all thy mind, and with all thy strength."   Mark 12:30

西门附近的斋宫是给皇帝斋戒的地方，他必须在此斋戒三天，才可去祭天。皇帝除了斋戒之外，还不可作乐，近女色，和审判罪案。他一定要先清心谦卑自己，才能去敬拜上帝。上帝是不会接受皇帝不以全心、全意、全性来敬拜祂的。

斋宫的前门，皇帝在斋宫内斋戒三天才去祭天

根据《论语》：「获罪于天，无所祷也。」[13]意思就是说：如果人冒犯了天，就没有什么可祷告了。

「我若心里注重罪孽，主必不听。」 诗篇66:18

「清心的人有福了！因为他们必得见上帝。」
马太福音5:8

「你要尽心，尽性，尽意，尽力爱主你的上帝。」
马可福音12:30

Exterior view of the Imperial Vault of Heaven

Interior view of the Imperial Vault of Heaven. The throne and tablet of Shang-Di are erected at the center

The Imperial Vault of Heaven 皇穹宇, located directly north of the Circular Mound Altar, was used exclusively to house the sacred tablets of Shang-Di and the ancestors of the royal family. Inside the Imperial Vault of Heaven, the throne at the center served as the shrine of Shang-Di. A tablet with Chinese and Manchu inscriptions engraved in gold is found erected upon this throne. These inscriptions read:

皇天上帝

or, "Heavenly Sovereign Shang-Di", with its equivalent translation in Manchu on the left side of the tablet.

Although the Manchurians were a small minority in China, they somehow managed to overthrow the Ming 明 Dynasty to establish the Qing/Ching 清 Dynasty. The Manchurians were not Han Chinese, yet they acknowledged Shang-Di

皇穹宇外景

皇穹宇内，上帝牌位放在中央高台

皇穹宇位于圆丘坛的北面，是专门放置上帝和皇族牌位的地方。在皇穹宇的正中间是上帝的宝座，宝座上放置了刻写着满汉文金字上帝的牌位－「皇天上帝」。

虽然满族是中国的少数民族，他们却推翻了明朝建立清朝。满族人非汉

as the Supreme God of the Universe!

We see here that Shang-Di is not only the Supreme God of the Chinese, but also the Supreme God of many of the neighboring peoples!

"Behold, I am the LORD, the God of all flesh: is there anything too hard for me?" Jeremiah 32:27

Close up view of Shang-Di's tablet, with the inscriptions engraved in Chinese and its equivalent in Manchu on the left

A Firewood Stove used to offer burnt sacrifices to Heaven

Outside the Gate to the Hall of Prayer for Good Harvests, stands a Fanchai Stove 燔柴爐, or Firewood Stove. It was here that the emperor would burn the sacrifices that his officials had prepared and slaughtered for him in the Butcher Pavilion. Displayed on top of this stove is a reproduction of a sacrificial ox.

41

族，然而他们承认上帝是宇宙至高的真神！

所以由此可见，上帝不单是中国人至高的真神，也是邻近许多民族的至高真神！

「我是耶和华，是凡有血气者的上帝，岂有我难成的事吗？」 耶利米书 32:27

皇天上帝牌位用满汉金字刻写而成

祈年殿外面放置的燔柴炉，是皇帝将在宰牲亭被宰杀和准备好给献祭用的牲畜烧掉的地方。今天燔柴炉上有一只用来献祭的牛的复制品供游客参观。

其实早在舜的时代已实行烧祭的仪式。舜在登基之时烧祭物来祭天，但是舜从哪儿学得向天烧祭物这习俗呢？

用来烧祭牲畜的燔柴炉

*"If any man of you bring an offering unto the LORD, you shall bring your offering of the **cattle**, even of the herd, and of the flock. If his offering be a **burnt sacrifice** of the herd, let him offer a male **without blemish**...and he shall put his hand upon the head of the burnt offering, and it shall be accepted for him to make atonement for him."*

Leviticus 1:2-4

The Hall of Prayer for Good Harvest

The Qiniandian 祈年殿, or Hall of Prayer for Good Harvests, was also known as Qigutan 祈穀壇, or the Altar of Prayer for Good Harvests. The entire structure was built one layer upon another without a single brick or nail. It is renowned as an architectural masterpiece around the world. The Hall of Prayer for Good Harvests was the sacred place where the emperors of the Ming and Qing dynasties prayed to Shang-Di for good harvests. Because China was an agricultural society for thousands of years, fruitful harvests were vital to the prosperity of the people.

The emperor openly acknowledged his dependence on the Heavenly Sovereign Shang-Di for his country's agricultural prosperity. According to the Bible, one way God reveals himself to other nations is through good harvests.

*"We also are men with like passions with you, and preach unto you that ye should turn from these vanities unto the living God, which made heaven, and earth, and the sea, and all things that are therein: Who in times past suffered all nations to walk in their own ways. **Nevertheless he left not himself without witness, in that he did good, and gave us rain from heaven, and fruitful seasons,** filling our hearts with food and gladness."*

Acts 14:15-17

Although in the past, God allowed all nations to *"walk in their own ways,"* yet he did not turn his back on them. He still gave them rain and fruitful harvests. It was Shang-Di who had provided for our needs throughout our five thousand years of Chinese history! It is Shang-Di who has made the Chinese the most populous people in the world!

43

「你们中间若有人献供物给耶和华，要从牛群羊群中，献牲畜为供物。他的供物若以牛为燔祭，就要在会幕门口献一只没有残疾的公牛，可以在耶和华面前蒙悦纳。他要按手在燔祭牲的头上，燔祭便蒙悦纳，为他赎罪。」

利未记 1:2-4

祈年殿外景

祈年殿又称祈谷坛，整座建筑以层叠式建成，没有用到一根钉子，一块砖石，是闻名全世界的建筑杰作。此处是明清两朝皇帝向上帝敬拜，祈求丰收的神圣之地。由于中国几千年来都以农立国，一年的丰收对百姓的生活来说至关重要。

皇帝公开承认他依赖皇天上帝，来赐百姓农产的富足。《圣经》也记述，上帝显现给各民族的一种方式，是赐给他们丰年。

「我们也是人，性情和你们一样。我们传福音给你们，是叫你们离弃这些虚妄，归向那创造天、地、海和其中万物的永生神。祂在从前的世代，任凭万国各行其道：然而为自己未尝不显出证据来，就如常施恩惠，从天降雨，赏赐丰年，叫你们饮食饱足，满心喜乐。」

使徒行传 14:15-17

过去上帝允许各民族「任意而行」，然而祂没有背弃他们，仍给他们雨水，谷物丰收。上帝供给中国人五千年来的需要，使中华民族成为世界上人口最多的民族！

Inside the Hall of Prayer for Good Harvests resides no idols but the throne of Shang-Di at the center. On top of this throne, the emperor placed the tablet of Shang-Di, which he took from the Imperial Vault of Heaven. It is the only known temple in all of China without an idol.

Interior of the Hall of Prayer for Good Harvests. There are no idols. The focus is the throne of Shang-Di. How eloquently this speaks of the one true God!

"Thou shalt not make unto thee any graven image (i.e. idols)"
Exodus 20:4

How did the Chinese know that Shang-Di accepted only blood and burnt sacrifices? How is it possible that the Chinese have a custom of offering sacrifices to Shang-Di so similar to the Jews' sacrifices to Jehovah? How did the Chinese know that they were NOT to make an idol of Shang-Di? We see here that the historical account found in the Holy Bible agrees amazingly well with the account found in Chinese history! These practices began with Noah's sacrifice to the God of Heaven upon exiting the ark after the Flood. The God of Christianity DID NOT ignore the Chinese for 5,000 years of their history! He has always been there, and has always left a witness of Himself that we might come to know Him personally.

祈年殿中没有放置偶像，只有上帝的宝座在中央，且在宝座上放置了从皇穹宇搬来的皇天上帝的牌位。它是全中国唯一一座没有偶像的庙宇。

祈年殿的内景。内只放置上帝宝座，
这是中国唯一没有放置偶像的庙宇

「不可为自己雕刻偶像，也不可做什么形象仿佛上天、下地和地底下、水中的百物。不可跪拜那些像，也不可事奉它……」　　　　　　　　　　　　　出埃及记20:4

中国人怎么知道上帝只接受血祭和燔祭呢？中国人为何在敬拜上帝的习俗上跟犹太人向耶和华献祭如此相似呢？中国人怎么知道不能为上帝造偶像呢？我们在此看见《圣经》的历史记述和中国历史奇妙吻合的地方。这些做法源于挪亚在洪水后，出方舟筑坛献祭而来。可见基督教的上帝在中国人五千年的历史中，一点也没有忽略他们。祂是常存的，并且更为自己在中国人中留下了见证，让人们来认识祂。

"Forasmuch then as we are the offspring of God, we ought not to think that the Godhead is like unto gold, or silver, or stone, graven by art and man's device. And the times of this ignorance God winked at; but now commandeth all men every where to repent: Because he hath appointed a day, in the which he will judge the world in righteousness by [that] man whom he hath ordained; [whereof] he hath given assurance unto all [men], in that he hath raised him from the dead."

Acts 17:29-31

In times past, God has allowed us to *"walk in our own ways"* by pursuing false religions, vain philosophies, and idol worship. He has overlooked our past ignorance that caused us to neglect worshipping Him as the one true God who can save us from our sins. But now He is commanding us to repent and receive His only begotten son Jesus Christ as our personal savior. There is no other way to restore a broken relationship with Shang-Di.

Even the Chinese character for righteousness 義 shows us the truth of how we can be made righteous in the sight of God.

羊 + 我 = 義

Lamb + I, me   righteousness

In the Chinese word "righteousness" 義, notice that the character for lamb 羊 is on top of the character for me 我. It is the lamb over me that makes me righteous! It is the lamb covering me, especially my sins, which makes me righteous! It is Jesus, the Lamb of God, who can bring us back to Shang Di. He is the only way back!

"The next day John seeth Jesus coming unto him, and saith, 'Behold, the Lamb of God which taketh away the sin of the world!'"   John 1:29

"Jesus saith unto him, 'I am the way, the truth, and the life, no man cometh unto the Father but by me'"   John 14:6

"That if thou shalt confess with thy mouth the Lord Jesus, and shalt believe in thine heart that God hath raised him from the dead, thou shalt be saved. For with the heart man believeth unto righteousness; and with the mouth confession is made unto salvation."   Romans 10:9-10

Qing/Ching 清 Dynasty

The beginning of the Qing Dynasty, which lasted from 1644 to 1911 A.D., marked the end of the Ming Dynasty. The Qing Dynasty was the last dynasty in Chinese history. The Qing emperors left the rituals and music associated with the annual sacrifice at the Altar of Heaven virtually unchanged from the Ming.

「我们既是上帝所生的，就不当以为上帝的神性像人用手艺、心思所雕刻的金、银、石。世人蒙昧无知的时候，上帝并不监察，如今却吩咐各处的人都要悔改。因为祂已经定了日子，要藉着祂所设立的人按公义审判天下，并且叫祂从死里复活，给万人作可信的凭据。」

使徒行传 17:29-31

过去，上帝任凭我们一意孤行去追求其它假的宗教，虚妄的学说和拜偶像，祂任凭我们无知地去忽视祂，不敬拜祂。但现在祂吩咐我们悔改，接受祂唯一的儿子耶稣基督为赎罪的羔羊、世人的救主；除此之外，没有其他方法能够恢复我们与上帝破碎的关系。

中国人的「義」字也见证这个《圣经》真理。

羊 ＋ 我 ＝ 義（义）

「我」在羔「羊」耶稣底下才有「義」（义）。主耶稣是上帝为我们预备的羔羊，祂是唯一挽救、恢复我们与上帝关系的「道」。

「次日，约翰看见耶稣来到他那儿，就说：看哪，上帝的羔羊，除去世人罪孽的！」

约翰福音 1:29

「耶稣说，我就是道路、真理、生命，若不藉着我，没有人能到父那里去。」

约翰福音 14:6

「你若口里认耶稣为主，心里信上帝叫祂从死里复活，就必得救。因为，人心里相信，就可以称义，口里承认，就可以得救。」

罗马书 10:9-10

清朝（公元后 1644 - 1911 年）

明朝之后的清朝是中国最后一个朝代。清朝皇帝基本上没有改变明朝每年在天坛祭天的祭礼和祭乐。

Emperor Kang Xi/Kang-Hsi 康熙

Emperor Kang Xi of the Qing Dynasty was considered one of the greatest and wisest emperors in Chinese history. He reigned from 1661 AD to 1722 A.D. During his reign, a controversy raged among the missionaries concerning the correct rendering of the Christian God into the Chinese language. The Jesuits wanted to use the terms Tian 天 and Shang-Di 上帝 for the one true God. The Dominicans and Franciscans objected. In fact, even one of the Catholic Bishops by the name Maigrot asserted that Heaven was a material thing and should not be worshipped. This controversy was eventually presented to Emperor Kang Xi, who issued the following statement:

> *"I had agreed with the formulation the Peking fathers (i.e. Jesuit Missionaries) had drawn up in 1700: that Confucius was honored by the Chinese as a master, but his name was not invoked in prayer for the purpose of gaining happiness, rank, or wealth; that worship of the ancestors was an expression of love and filial remembrance, not intended to bring protection to the worshiper; and that there was no idea, when an ancestral tablet was erected, that the soul of the ancestor dwelt in the tablet. And when sacrifices were offered to Heaven it was not the blue existent sky that was addressed, but **the Lord and Creator of all things**. If the ruler Shang-Di (上帝) was sometimes called Heaven, Tien (天), that had no more significance than giving honorific names to the emperor."[14]*

Later, when Kang Xi was pressured by missionaries to accept baptism, *"he always excused himself by saying that he worshipped the same God as the Christians."* [15]We see that Emperor Kang Xi understood that both Shang-Di 上帝 and Heaven 天 to stand for the one Supreme Being, the same one true God of Christianity!

Conclusion

From our brief study of Chinese history, we can clearly see that the Supreme God Shang-Di 上帝 has always left himself a witness from the very beginning to the present day. He wants us to know him personally. He has never ignored nor forsaken the Chinese people. He is the sovereign God who has created all things, and has made the Chinese the most populous people group in the world. God must love the Chinese very much! Throughout our history, we drank from the river of God's abundant blessing. The famous Chinese proverb 飲水思源 literally means *"when you drink water, remember the source"*. We have taken Shang-Di's abundant blessings, but we have neglected and forgotten him.

康熙皇帝（公元后 1661- 1722 年）

康熙皇帝被视为中国历史中伟大又智慧的君王之一，在位六十一年。当他在位时，西洋宣教士因如何正确地使用中文来翻译《圣经》中真神的名字而起了争议。耶稣会（Jesuits）教士想用「天」和「上帝」来命名至高无上的神，但道明会（Dominicans）和方济会（Franciscans）的教士却反对。事实上，天主教一位名为梅格特（Magrot）的主教坚称「天」不过是一种物质，不应去礼拜它。这个争论最后呈到了康熙那儿，康熙发表看法如下：

> 「我同意北京神甫们（即耶稣会教士）在 1700 年形成的看法，即孔子是令中国人敬仰的老师，但在祷告中，本没有用他的名字去求名利、地位或幸福的；而对于祖先的敬拜只是爱与孝心的追念，不在于求保护。至于祖先牌位的设立，并不具有祖先神灵住在其中的意念。同样地，在向天献祭的时候，对象不是蓝天，而是创造万物的主。如果上帝有时被称为「天」，那就与有时给皇帝另一个尊称无异。」[14]

后来宣教士们施压康熙接受浸礼，「他总是说他与基督徒所敬拜的是同一位上帝而推辞掉。」[15] 由此可见康熙皇帝明白「上帝」跟「天」是同一位唯一创造宇宙全能的真神，也就是基督徒所敬拜的上帝！

结论

从这简短对中国历史的研讨中，我们可以清楚看见，至高的上帝从中国文明的开始，直到今天，在中国历史和文化中替自己留下了见证，使我们可以亲自认识祂。祂没有忽视或遗弃中国人。祂是创造万物的至高全能真神，并使中国人成为全世界人口最多的人种，祂一定非常爱中国人！贯穿历史，我们饮于上帝丰富祝福的泉源。中国有名的成语「饮水思源」让我们反省：我们获取上帝丰富的祝福，却忽视且忘记祂了。

Man was created to worship and have fellowship with his Creator God. When we cannot or will not do that, we will very quickly find other things to fill the spiritual void in our lives, but they never can. Only the one true Creator God, Shang-Di, can fill the deepest needs in the human heart!

Throughout our history, we have pursued vain philosophies and religions through Buddhism, Taoism, Atheism, ancestral worship, agnosticism, idol worship, and the mere worship of human beings whom we made into gods. We have turned our backs on our true roots in Shang-Di. It is time to once again acknowledge the true source of all our blessings in the eternal God Shang-Di.

Will you return to your true spiritual roots now in the Eternal God, Shang-Di? Shang-Di sent His one and only begotten Son, Jesus Christ, to die on the cross for all our sins. God did not ignore the Chinese for 5,000 years of their history. Christianity is not a western religion. Will you repent of your sins and put your faith in Shang-Di now? Will you follow Jesus as the only way back to God?

Imagine a good father and his child. He faithfully takes care of the child and supplies him with everything he needs to grow up and become a strong healthy adult. What a beautiful thing to watch this relationship between father and child and see their love grow for each other over the years. Imagine that child coming home one day and telling the father, "You didn't do anything for me. Everything I have and everything I've become I've done with my own hard work. I don't need you and I don't want anything to do with you anymore!" Truly such a child would be guilty of "Drinking water and forgetting the source" of that life giving blessing!

But my dear friend, haven't you been guilty of the same transgression by turning your back on Shang Di? Haven't you ignored the fact that He is the true source of your life? Have you forgotten all the good things and blessings God gave you over your lifetime? Do you worship and thank Him every day? A Chinese proverb says, "If you do not worship heaven above, He will send down calamities upon the people 弗敬上天，降災下民." If you are guilty of worshipping false gods and not worshipping Shang-Di, then you too are guilty of "drinking the water of life but forgetting the true source."

So what can you do now? What must you do to be saved from the consequences of having committed such a serious transgression? A Chinese proverb says, "They who are in accord with Heaven are preserved, and they who rebel against Heaven perish 順天者昌，逆天者亡."

There is only one thing we can do. Shang-Di has made it very clear that we must each personally receive, by faith, Jesus Christ as our Savior and LORD. Only He can save us from the penalty of our sin (i.e. going to hell forever). Shang-Di knows your heart. He knows if you are truly sorry and repentant for the

人类被上帝创造就是要来敬拜创造他的上帝，并且与祂有深交。一旦我们失去了这个关系，我们会很快去寻求其它的东西来填满生命中灵性的真空。但这些东西根本无法满足人心灵的空乏，只有唯一创造万物的真神才能满足人心最深处的需求！

我们从中国历史看出，我们曾追寻空虚的哲理和藉着佛教、道教、无神论、祖先崇拜、不可知论、拜偶像、以及将人升格为神等方式，来填补灵性的真空。这些做法使中国人离弃自己的根本，就是造他的上帝。现在是回归并承认赐给我们生命和祝福的永恒真神上帝的时候了。

你愿意现在回到你真正的灵性根本，永恒的真神上帝面前吗？上帝差遣祂的独生子耶稣基督为我们所有的罪死在十字架上，在中国人五千年的历史中，祂没有忘记或忽视我们。基督教不是西方宗教（洋教，红毛教）。你现在愿意悔改你的罪，相信上帝吗？你愿意追随耶稣，承认祂是那条回到上帝唯一的道路吗？

想像一对父子。父亲忠实地照顾儿子，供给他成长所需要的一切，帮助他长大成人。父子在多年来生活中，培养出美好爱的关系。假想一天儿子返家对父亲说：「你什么都没有为我做，我拥有的一切都是靠自己努力得来的。我不需要你，以后也跟你无关！」这样的孩子是不是违背了「饮水思源」呢？

但是亲爱的朋友，你是否也离弃上帝，犯了同样的过错呢？你是否忽视这位赐你生命的真神？你忘记了一生中上帝赐给你的一切福分吗？你每天敬拜并感谢祂吗？中国有一句成语说「弗敬上天，降灾下民」。假如你崇拜假神，离弃真神，你也犯了没有「饮水思源」的罪。

你该怎么办呢？犯下这么严重的过错能如何获救呢？中国有另一句成语说「顺天者昌，逆天者亡」。

我们唯一能做的一件事，就是上帝清楚吩咐的：每人以信心接受耶稣作我们的救主和生命的主，只有祂能拯救我们不受罪

transgressions you committed against him. If you are, then you can pray and ask His forgiveness and ask Jesus Christ to come into your heart and cleanse you from all your sins.

> *"But as many as received him (Jesus), to them gave he (Shang-Di) power to become the sons of God, even to them that believe on his name: Which were born, not of blood, nor of the will of the flesh, nor of the will of man, but of God."*
> John 1:12-13

> *"Behold, I (Jesus) stand at the door and knock. If anyone hears my voice and opens the door, I will come in to him and dine with him, and he with me."*
> Revelations 3:20

Jesus Christ is asking you to open the door of your heart. Would you like to repent of your sins now and ask Jesus Christ to come into your life? The following is a suggested prayer:

> *"Heavenly Father, I realize now that you are the true source of all the blessings in my life. I never thanked you as I should have. I've never worshipped you as the one true God of all creation. Yet you still blessed me. I realize that my sin deserves to be punished. I believe that you sent your only begotten son, the Lord Jesus Christ, to die on the cross for my sins. I know I am a sinner. I believe you died for me and resurrected from the dead. I trust in you alone as my Savior. I open the door of my heart and life to receive you as my Savior and Lord. Thank you for forgiving my sins and giving me eternal life. In Jesus' Name, Amen."*

Does this prayer express the desires of your heart? If so, please pray this prayer right now and give your life to the LORD Jesus Christ. If you have prayed this prayer, or would like someone to lead you through this prayer, please contact us.

If you are interested in learning more about your Chinese roots, or about how to become a Christian, please give us a call. There are two other booklets in this series: "Who is Shang-Di?" and "China's Blood Covenant with Shang-Di." Thank you for taking the time to read this booklet.

的惩罚（下地狱）。上帝知道你的心，祂知道你是否诚心悔改你对祂犯下的过错。你若诚心，就可祷告祈求祂赦免你，并邀请耶稣进入你心中，洁净你一切的罪。

> 「凡接待祂的，就是信祂名的人，祂就赐他们权柄，作上帝的儿女。这等人不是从血肉气生的，不是从情欲生的，也不是从人意生的，乃是从上帝生的。」
>
> 约翰福音 1:12-13

> 耶稣说：「看哪，我站在门外叩门。若有听见我声音就开门的，我要进到他那里去，我与他，他与我一同坐席。」
>
> 启示录 3:20

耶稣邀请你向祂打开心门，你愿意现在就悔改你的罪，请祂进到你的生命里来吗？下面是一个建议性的祷告：

> 「创造天地的上帝啊，我知道祢是赐福我生命的源头，但是我从来不知道感谢祢。祢也是创造我的上帝，我也从来不知道要敬拜祢。我知道自己有罪，我的罪该得惩罚。但是我相信祢差遣耶稣为我死了，而且祂从死里复活，为我战胜了死亡，我现在信靠耶稣作我的救主，谢谢祂在十架上为我付出的罪的代价。我现在将心门打开，接受祢为我预备的救恩。谢谢祢赦免我的罪孽，把永生赐给我。我奉耶稣的名来到祢面前祷告，阿门。」

这个祷告是否表达你内心的愿望？如果是，你现在就可以这样祷告。如果你已经作过这个祷告，或是需要他人带领你来作这个祷告，那么请与你的带领人联络。

如果你想多知道有关中国人的信仰根源，或如何成为基督徒，请与我们联络！在此信仰寻根系列中还有两本小册子：《上帝是谁》和《圣爱盟约》，欢迎你索取，并谢谢你花时间阅读这本小册子。

Contact Information:
Chinese Resource Ministry (AFC)
Email: CRM@afcinc.org
Website: http://www.ChineseResourceMinistry.org
Telephone: 1-888-999-7959

    If you have difficulty with evolutionism and creationism, there are many online resources that can help you. Please look up the following research materials:
http://www.answersingenesis.org
http://www.icr.org
http://www.creation.com

Chinese Spiritual Roots:
http://www.ocf.berkeley.edu/~davytong/publications/

https://goo.gl/1hhj5S

https://goo.gl/qNQTGX

    You may also contact the person or church group that gave you this pamphlet at the following address:

Printed in Canada

我们的联络方法是：

福音资源事工 Chinese Resource Ministry (AFC)

电子邮件：CRM@afcinc.org

网址：http://www.ChineseResourceMinistry.org

电话：1-888-999-7959

    若你对进化论及创造论有些问题感到困难，网络中有许多资料可以帮助你。以下的一些网页有很多最新研究资料：

http://www.answersingenesis.org

http://www.icr.org

http://www.creation.com

中国人的信仰根源-

http://www.ocf.berkeley.edu/~davytong/publications/

https://goo.gl/1hhj5S   https://goo.gl/qNQTGX

发送本册子者的个人联络资料：

References

[1] James Legge as translator, *The Chinese Classics*, Vol. III, *Shoo King (Shu Jing)*, Taipei: South Materials Center reprint 1983, pp. 23.

[2] Ibid., pp. 26.

[3] Ibid., pp. 33-35.

[4] Ibid., pp.511.

[5] Pei-Jung, Fu, *On Religious Ideas of the Pre-Chou China*, Article from Chinese Culture: A Quarterly Review, Vol. XXVI, Number 3, September, 1985 (Yang Ming Shan, Taiwan: the China Academy: the Institute for Advanced Chinese Studies, 1985) pp.23-39.

[6] James Legge as translator, *The Chinese Classics*, Vol. III, *Shoo King (Shu Jing)*, Taipei: South Materials Center reprint 1983, pp. 269. See also commentary on pp. 269.

[7] Ibid., pp. 315-316.

[8] James Legge, *The Notions of the Chinese Concerning God and Spirits*, Taipei: Ch'eng Wen Publishing Co, reprint 1971, pp.45.

[9] Ibid., pp. 44-49.

[10] Ibid., pp. 44-46.

[11] James Legge as translator, *Chinese Classics*, Vol. I & II, *Confucian Analects* (論語), Book III, Chapter XI, pp. 158.

[12] John Ross, *The Original Religion of China*, New York, Eaton and Mains, 1909, pp. 295-297.

[13] James Legge as translator, *Chinese Classics*, Vol. I & II, *Confucian Analects* (論語), Book III, Chapter XIII, pp. 159

[14] Jonathan D. Spence, *Emperor of China: Self-Portrait of K'ang-hsi,* New York: Alfred A. Knopf 1974, pp. 79-85

[15] Herbert A. Giles, *Religions of Ancient China*, Freeport, New York: Books for Libraries Press 1969, Reprint of the 1905 edition, pp. 17-18.

注解：

1 《书经》：帝曰：「畴咨若时登庸？」放齐曰：「胤子朱启明。」帝曰：「吁！嚚讼，可乎？」

2 《书经》：帝曰，「明明扬侧陋。」师锡帝曰：「有鳏在下，曰虞舜。」帝曰：「俞！予闻，如何？」岳曰：「瞽子，父顽，母嚚，象傲；克谐，以孝烝烝，乂不格奸。」

3 「堙」这个字就是「圜丘」的意思。后来天坛内的圜丘坛源于舜的「堙」。根据《书经》：肆类于上帝，禋于六宗，望于山，遍于群神。

4 《书经》：古之人迪惟有夏，乃有室大竞，籲俊尊上帝。

5 Pei-Jung Fu，On Religious Ideas of the Pre-Chou China，Article from Chinese Culture：A Quarterly Review，Vol.14，Number 3，September，1985（Yang Ming Shan, Taiwan：the China Academy：the Institute for Advanced Chinese Studies，1985）PP.23-39

6 根据司马迁《史记。殷本纪》：武乙無道，為偶人，謂之天神，舆之博，令人為行，天神不勝，乃僇辱之，為革囊盛血，仰而射之，命曰射天。**武乙獵於河渭之間，暴雷，武乙震死**。James Legge as translator，The Chinese Classics，Vol.3，ShooKing（Shu Jing），Taipei：South Materials Center reprint1983，pp.269. See also commentary on PP.269.

7 《书经》周书，武成，十节：列爵惟五，分土惟三，建官惟贤，位事惟能，重民五教，惟食丧祭…

8 James Legge，The Notions of the Chinese Concerning God and Spirits，Taipei：Ch'eng Wen Publishing Co，reprint 1971，PP.45.根据 Legge 参考唐朝历史记录：自周衰，禮樂壞于戰國，而廢絕于秦。

9 根据《大明会典》：自秦立四時，以祀白青黄赤四帝，汉高祖因之，增北時，以礼黑帝，至武帝，有雍五時，及渭阳五帝，甘泉太乙之祠，而昊天上帝之祭，则未嘗奉行，魏晋以後，宗鄭玄者，以为天有六名，歳凡丸祭，宗王肃者，以为天礼惟一，安得有六，一歲二祭，安得有九，虽因革不同，大抵多参二家之说。

10 同上。

11 《论语》，八佾第三，十一章

12 John Ross，The Original Religion of China，New York，Eaton and Mains，1909，PP.295-2977. John Ross 被允许在清朝祭天现场观察。

13 《论语》，八佾第三，十三章

14 译意 Jonathan D. Spence，Emperor of China：Self-Portrait of K'ang-hsi，New York：Alfred A. Knopf，1974，PP.79-85

15 Herbert A. Giles，Religions of Ancient China，Freeport，New York：Books for Libraries Press 1969，Reprint of the 1905 edition，PP.17-18